LAUNCH FUNNEL Affiliates

ERIC PEREZ

Copyright © 2018 Eric Perez

All rights reserved.

ISBN: **198675586X**
ISBN-13: **978-1986755863**

DISCLAIMER AND TERMS OF USE

This publication is copyrighted. All Rights Reserved. Unauthorized Reproduction is Strictly Prohibited. The information contained in this publication and the accompanying materials is for general information purposes only. While we endeavor to keep the information up-to-date and correct, we make no representations or warranties of any kind, express or implied, about the completeness, accuracy, reliability, effectiveness, suitability or availability with respect to this publication or the information, products, services, related graphics, or any contents contained in this publication for any purpose. Any reliance you, the reader, place on such information is therefore strictly at your own risk. If you wish to apply ideas contained in this publication, you are taking full responsibility for your actions. We disclaim any warranties (express or implied), merchantability, or fitness for any particular purpose. In no event will we be liable for any loss or damage including but not limited to; indirect or consequential loss or damage, or any loss or damage whatsoever arising from loss of data or profits stemming from or in connection with the use of this publication. We cannot guarantee results as results will differ from person to person and will depend on the effort taken. You are taking the decision to try these methods, and there are no guarantees to your success. Nor are we responsible for any of your actions. As always, the advice of a competent legal, tax, accounting or other professional should be sought. We do not warrant the performance, effectiveness or applicability of any methods or sites listed or linked to in this publication. If you purchase some items through the links provided, we may earn a commission. You will not pay more when buying a product through the links provided. In fact, you may be buying at a lower rate (or the author and publisher can provide bonuses) not vailable elsewhere. No part of this publication may be reproduced, copied, transmitted by any means, or changed in any format, sold, or used in any way other than what is outlined within this publication under any circumstances. Violations of this copyright will be enforced to the fullest extent of the law. Logos and trademarks mentioned in this guide are the property of their respective owners

All Rights Reserved

This information is for your eyes only. This eBook is for your own personal use and is not to be given away, traded, or distributed without the written consent of Eric Perez. This eBook does not come with and resell rights whatsoever. There are no guarantees of any kind, especially no income guarantees and you agree that our company is not responsible for the success or failure of your business decisions relating to any information presented by our company, or our company products or services. This eBook is to remain strictly in your sole possession

CONTENTS

Introduction 7

Overview of the System 8

Offer Selection 10

Tracking Account Setup 13

Spying Tactics 16

Keyword Research 21

Campaign Tracking Setup 26

Bing Campaign Setup 29

Campaign Monitoring and Optimization 35

Outsourcing 39

Conclusion 40

Resources 41

Introduction

First and foremost we want to congratulate you for picking up Launch Funnel Affiliates (let's refer to it as LFA from now on).

The system is focused on Bing and using a very unique yet powerful strategy to send dirt-cheap clicks to profitable offers.

The thing about Bing is that a lot of people know about it, but they don't know how to use it properly...

Which is why we are super excited that you put your trust in LFA!

Regardless of your experience or even knowledge when it comes to making money online, we are going to walk you through every single step of creating profitable Clickbank campaigns.

You literally can't get this type of quality *traffic* anywhere else.

The only thing we ask of you is to take some serious and massive action.

Making money online isn't all that hard, but it does require action and without action, nothing happens.

Here's to helping you make Clickbank commissions using LFA.

Thanks for being an awesome customer and enjoy!

Overview of the System

Before we dive in head first, we want to give you a brief bird's eye view of our system so you understand exactly what we're doing from start to finish.

The method is simple in nature, as we're about to show you.

The steps are as follows:

1. Find offers that should convert well for us

The first step is picking an offer that we want to promote. This is quite easy. We will talk you through the platforms we use and show you what simple indicators to use which will ensure you pick a good offer.

2. Spy to see the popular keywords and ads

Why re-invent the wheel? This step involves seeing the keywords and ad copy that the people running the offers themselves are using. This serves as a really good starting point. We show you the spy tools to you use to get you moving.

3. Determine our keywords for the offer

This is a simple step yet crucial. Our method is all about cheap clicks- and getting as many of them as we can. We recommend at least 1000 keywords for campaign. Don't worry, with our methods, it's easy to find a lot of the right keywords for the job.

4. Determine ad copies for the offer

This just involves a few minutes of research initially, and we walk you right through it.

5. Set up our campaign in Bing

This is our machine. With this, we will be getting eyeballs to offers that will pay us commissions when people buy. Put simply, we are looking to get as many eyeballs for the lowest price to the offers. It's as simple as that. You won't have to worry about blowing a budget or losing tons of money because the clicks are so cheap that even one or two sales gives you a massive return on investment.

6. Observe, tweak, profit

It's time to see how our machines are performing. Any machine needs to be well oiled to bring you maximum profits. Apply our simple steps to fine tune your machines for higher return on investment, with or without advanced tracking.

Offer Selection

The idea here is that I want to kind of walk you through my thought process, when it comes to picking an offer.

Now before we begin I want to clear up something very important.

What I'm going to show you in this section when it comes to affiliate marketing, the more competition, the better, okay?

You might have heard the opposite of that before but it's just not that way. If you see a lot of people promoting something, there's a reason why and it's because they are making a lot of money...

And there's no reason why you can't go in there and make a lot of money too.

So now that I've gotten that out of the way, we are going to be using Clickbank offers for this system so make sure you sign up for Clickbank if you haven't already.

Once you sign up to Clickbank you are going to want to go to the marketplace tab on the top and then click Advanced Search (as shown on the next page).

After you click on Advanced Search, simply click on Search on the next page

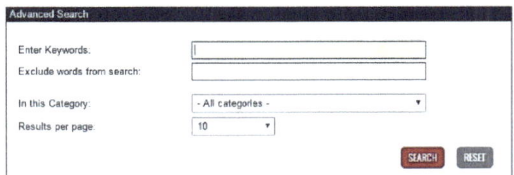

Lastly, you'll want to sort by Gravity so that you can see all of the current hottest offers.

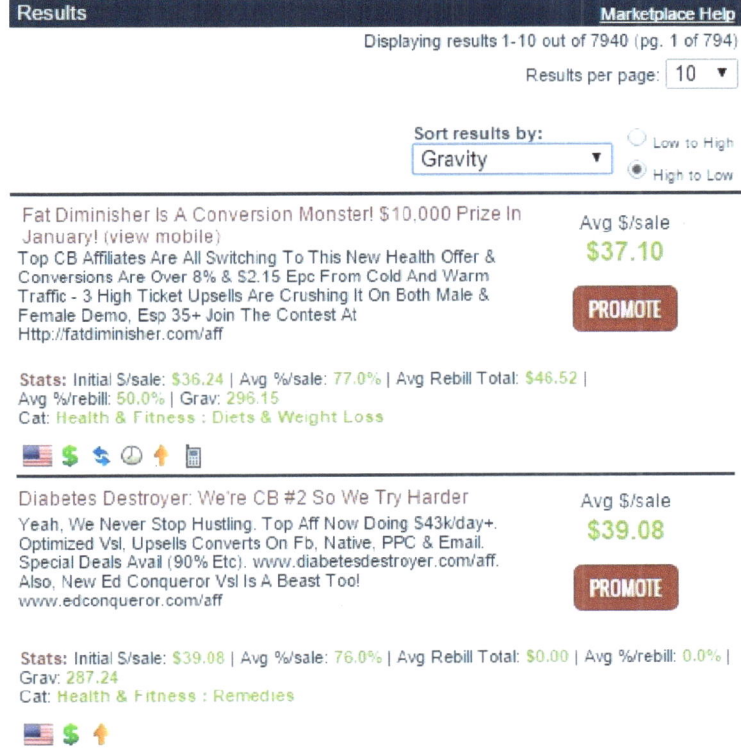

So now that you know the top offers, here is one of the

important factors you want to look for when it comes to promoting a product: Avg $/sale. Obviously since you are going to be sending cheap clicks to an offer, you can keep that factor low...

But what you can't always control is the average sale because depending on how the vendor sets up the funnel.

What you can control is whether or not your promote an offer, and that's why you want to go with offers that have at least $30.

The next factor you want to look for (that a lot of people miss out on) are the direct benefits of being an affiliate. If you take a look at many of the affiliate pages that are given in the description of offers, many of them offer incentives for you to promote.

For example, some offers will give you a bump to 90% commissions after making 10 sales, some will give you a $100 bonus after making 10 sales, and sometimes even both (which is really cool)!

So keep that in mind, that even if you were to say lose $50 on making 10 sales, PLUS you got a $100 bonus and a HUGE bump on commissions, that's an absolutely massive advantage compared to any other affiliate out there.

Another factor you want to look for is tools. Tools can make your life SO much easier when it comes to promoting an offer as many times they will give you keywords, copy for ad campaigns, landing pages, swipes, demographics, and so much more. And that's basically it!

So keep in mind that when you're looking for an offer, you want to look at the competition (gravity), Avg $/sale, extra bonuses for promoting, and affiliate tools to make your life easier.

Tracking Account Setup

So, before we begin with tracking, you need to know that it's 100% optional.

Our method is about cheap clicks, which means we aren't overly concerned with tweaking and optimization every step of the way.

However, we wanted to give you the option since you can still optimize your campaign by seeing which keywords brought you the sale, and a bunch more information about your campaign like locations, device type used, etc. This section will show you our favorite tracking tool, which does have a price tag of $100 per month.

However, you can get a 30 day trial for just $1 to see how you like it.

I will now walk you through the steps to setting up your tracking account.

1) Head to www.funnelflux.com and sign up for your free trial.

2) Set up your account, following instructions inside for how to install funnel flux on your server. For quick reference, this is the video that you need to follow (the license and files you need will be in your funnel flux account) - https://www.youtube.com/watch?v=OpU3cq-F6CA

3) Once inside funnel flux, it should look something like this:

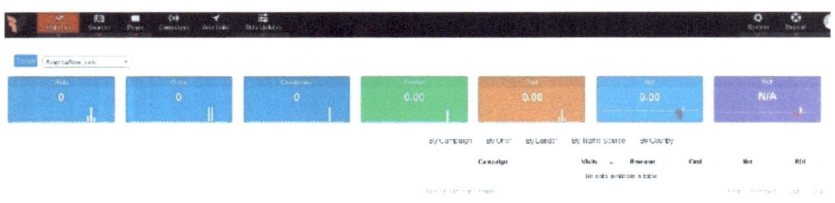

4) The next step is to input a few settings for our system. So once inside, click sources up at the top, then head to "Traffic Sources". Once there, hit "New Traffic Source" and input the following information.

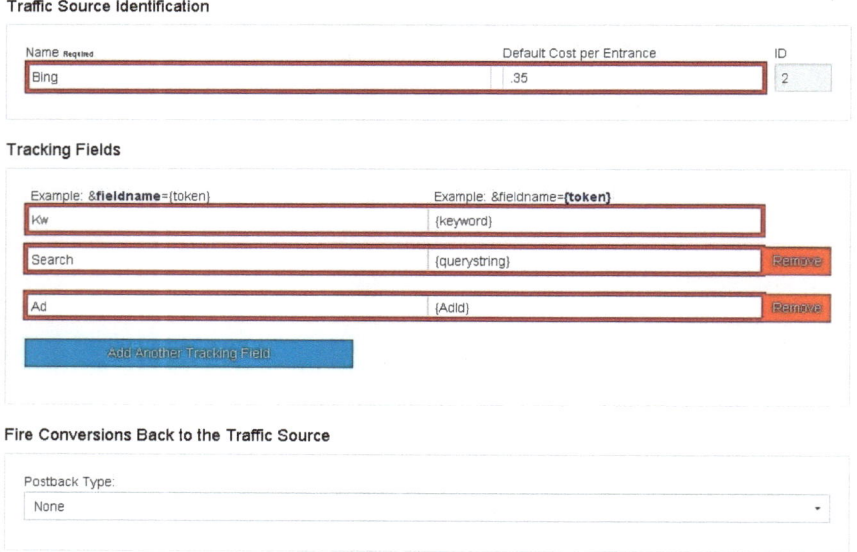

5) Once you have completed step 4, head to Sources in the top left again, but this time to "Offer Sources". Select "New Offer Source" and input the name of the main network you want to use. Since we're primarily choosing our offers from Clickbank, you can simply enter "Clickbank" as your offer

source.

6) The last thing we need to do is establish a partnership between Clickbank and your Funnel Flux tracking account. This is actually simple and is already explained in this video: https://www.youtube.com/watch?v=gklZWm_zCIw

7) Now, we have our tracking set up so that we can go in and create tracking campaigns. We will be showing how to do this in a later Module. You can leave this as it for now.

Spying Tactics

The idea of this section is that you want to go into your campaign with as much intel as possible (so that you have the greatest chances for success).

Think about it, a LOT of affiliates out there are running campaigns that are super profitable, and what that means is that you can go out there and get a good glimpse of what's working.

Why try and reinvent the wheel, right?

So I'm going to grab a high converting offer and show you the websites that I utilize to properly spy on what others are doing.

The first site is called https://www.ispionage.com (be sure to sign up for free version).

Once you get your free account, you can enter in the website of the Clickbank offer that you want to promote.

In this case it's going to be 3weekdiet.com as shown in the next picture.

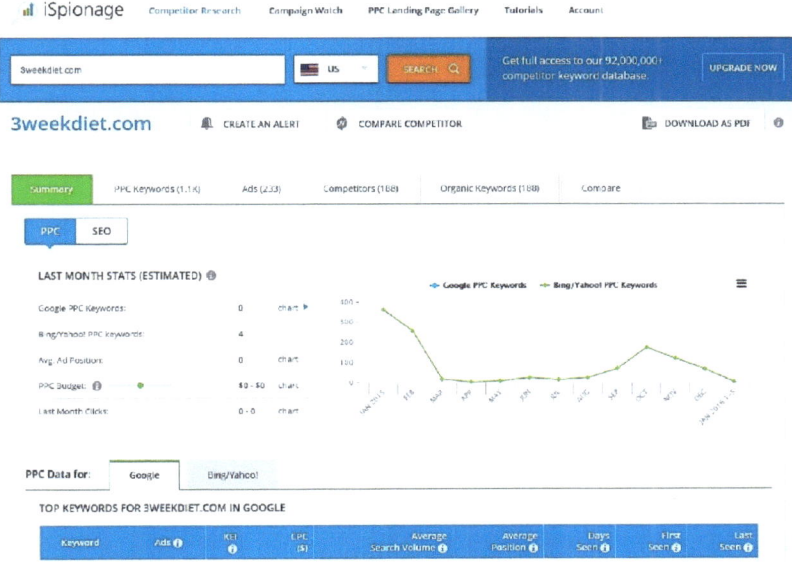

If you click on the PPC Keywords and then the Bing/Yahoo tab that opens up, you're going to see that there's ALOT of keywords being shown (which is what we are looking for).

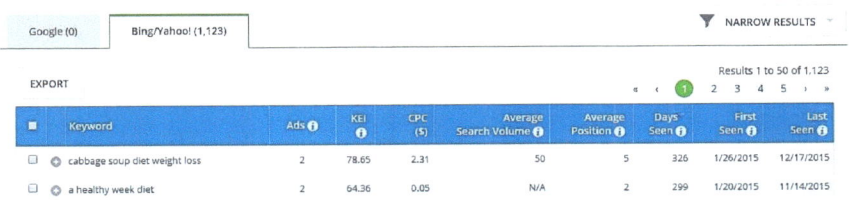

So that's one site to spy on offers, another one that is free (you just have to sign up for) is http://www.follow.net

Same thing as Ispionage we are going to type in the website of the offer that we are going to promote, using 3weekdiet.com again.

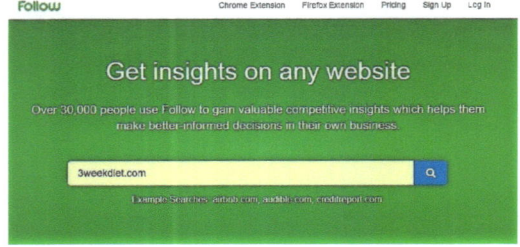

Once you type that in there and hit enter, you are looking for similar data to confirm that affiliates are constantly promoting this offer.

Aside from that, the great thing about follow.net is that it gives you even more tools to work with such as keywords, top keywords, and ad copy.

To get the best intel you'd obviously need to invest in that, but we're not exactly focused on that, just what they have to offer you for free so that you can confirm that offer that you are going to promote is profitable.

Pretty straightforward, right?

And the last spot we have to spy on the competition, is a site you'll probably NEVER guess in a million years... Bing.com ;)

Simply hop on over to Bing.com and type in 3 week diet.

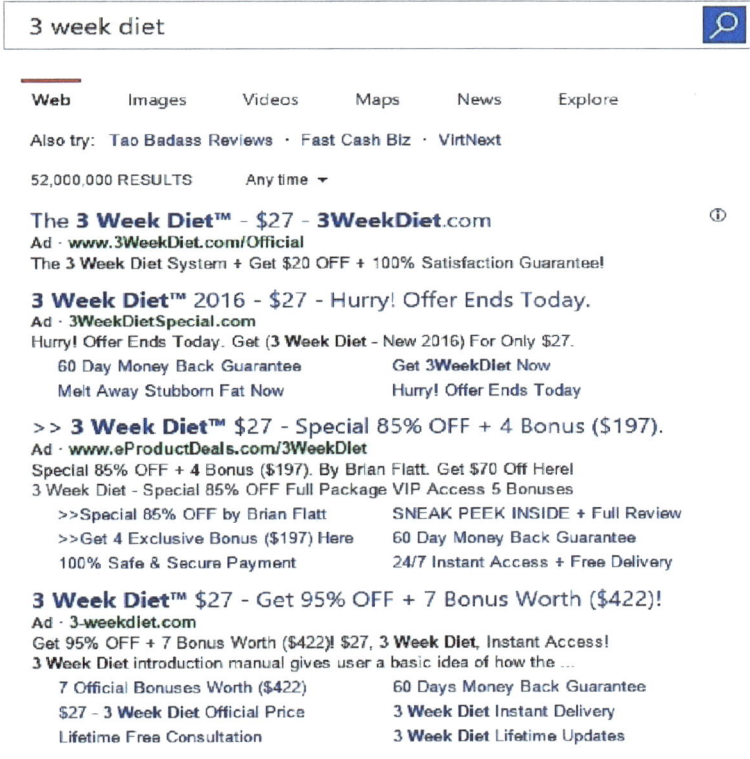

And what do we have here?
Notice how all of the ad spots are decorated with the 3 Week Diet?

Consider that another good sign that this offer has the green light.

So let's wrap up this section, in 3 simple steps.

1) Check Ispionage
2) Check Follow.net
3) Check Bing

If not you notice all of these sources have a bunch of ads for the offer you are 22 going to promote.

If not, then you might want to consider promoting a different offer.

Remember, competition is your best friend.

Keyword Research

This section is crucial to your success, and is the difference between something saying "Oh I'm not getting any clicks" and the person who is getting very cheap clicks and driving home the commissions.

Now, this system is based upon using a very large volume of keywords...

However the problem is that most people don't know where to get those keywords, and this section is going to solve that problem.

The first spot you are going to look for keywords is in the affiliate page of each offer.

Now if you search for surveys in Clickbank you will come across an offer called Paid Surveys At Home.

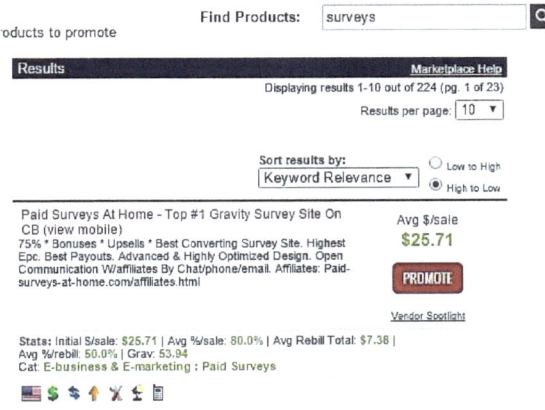

Simply copy and paste their link for affiliates shown in the bottom part of their 24 description there and that will take you to their tools.

Check out the keywords they are giving you here:

Now keep in mind this is just random offer and that not every single affiliate page is going to give you these keywords, but it certainly doesn't hurt to look!

So that's one area to find keywords that you are going to use, let's move onto the next which is Google Keyword Planner (you will need a free google account).

On the main page, you are going to want to click on search for new keyword and ad group ideas.

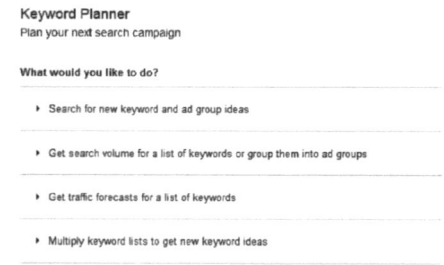

Once you click on that simply enter 2 or 3 keywords to get more ideas.

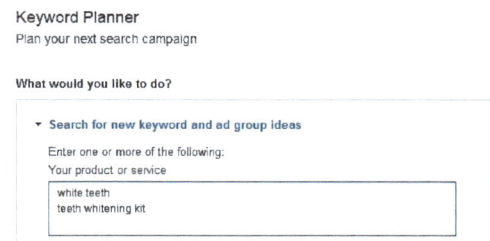

Don't worry about anything else then click on Get ideas.

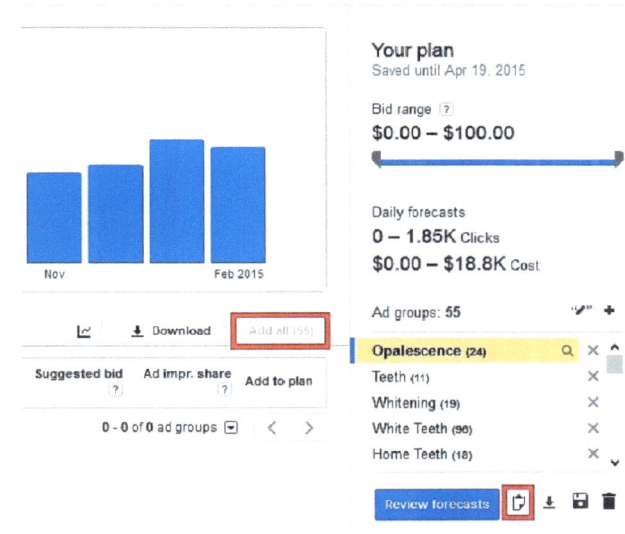

Then you are going to want to click on Add all (in red on left) then click on the copy simple (in red on right) and you can copy those to notepad.

You now have a TON of keywords to put back into your campaign.

So let's look at this last and little-known source: https://neilpatel.com/ubersuggest (Ubbersuggest).

All you have to do here is enter in one of your keywords and then you will get a ton of similar keyword variations.

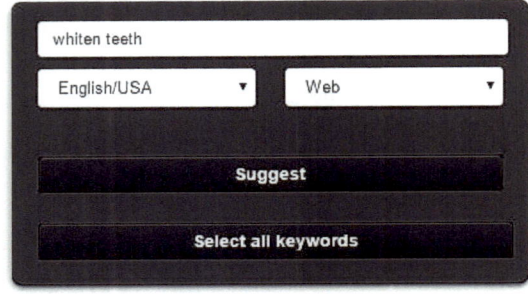

Now check out all of the keywords you're going to get below it.

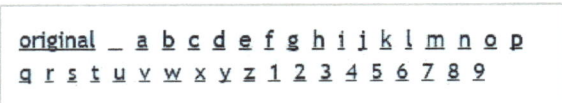

⇧ whiten teeth

- whiten teeth
- whiten teeth fast
- whiten teeth photoshop
- whiten teeth with baking soda
- whiten teeth with braces
- whiten teeth with banana peel
- whiten teeth with charcoal
- whiten teeth with strawberries
- whiten teeth in photo
- whiten teeth home remedy

⇧ whiten teeth +

- whiten teeth fast
- whiten teeth at home
- whiten teeth photoshop
- whiten teeth with baking soda
- whiten teeth with braces
- whiten teeth with banana peel
- whiten teeth at home fast
- whiten teeth with charcoal
- whiten teeth with strawberries
- whiten teeth in photo

And the best part is that there are even more keywords

in each of those groups if you click on the green + sign.

So once you have all of those, all you need to do is go back up to the top and click on Select all keywords and they will appear on the right side of the page.

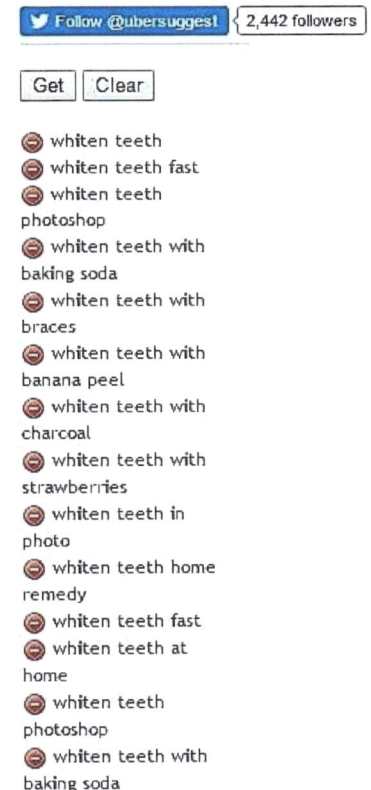

Simply click the Get button and you can copy all of them onto a Notepad file to save, easy stuff right? So let's recap.

You can get keywords from specific affiliate tools pages, Google Keyword planner, and Ubersuggest.

Now on to the good stuff.

Campaign Tracking Setup

By this point, you have all the components for your campaign ready.

If you want to track the campaign, which would allow you to see which keywords brought sales and which keywords did not (along with conversion information based on location, device used, etc.) then follow this section to set up your campaign tracking.

The first thing we need to do is add our offer to funnel flux.

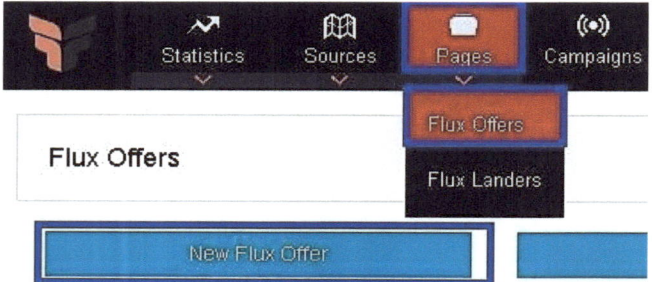

Enter in the information to all of the following fields...

Next, we need to set up our campaign.

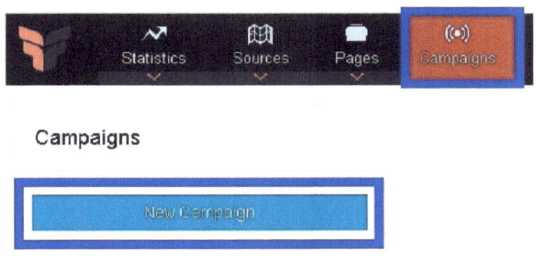

Enter your campaign name and then click save, from there create your funnel.

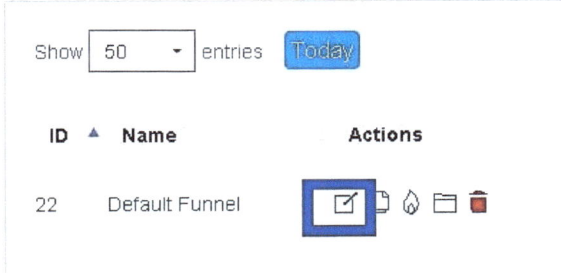

Add your flux offer by right clicking

Once you add the flux offer, just click on the little orange circle in traffic and drag it to the circle in the flux offer, so now your campaign should look like this.

Funnel Diagram

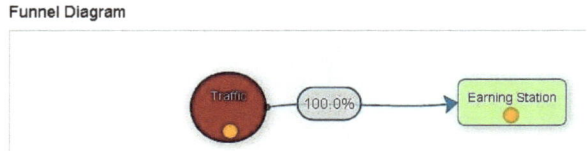

Our campaign is now set up for proper tracking.

To get our link for our Bing campaign, we go to "Your Link" at the top and fill in the appropriate selections to get our link.

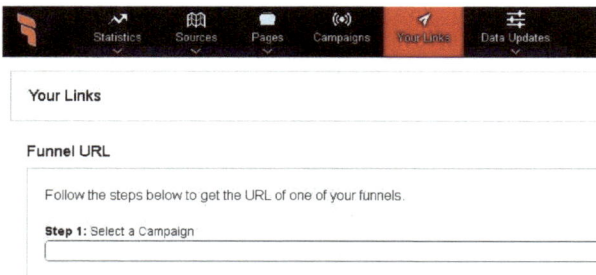

We are ready to set up our Bing campaign now!

Bing Campaign Setup

By this point, we have

- Our offer
- Our keywords
- Our ad copy
- Our offer link (or tracking link)

It's time to set up our first commission machine! (Bing campaign).

First, log into your Bing ads account www.bingads.com

Next, from the main screen, we want to create a new campaign.

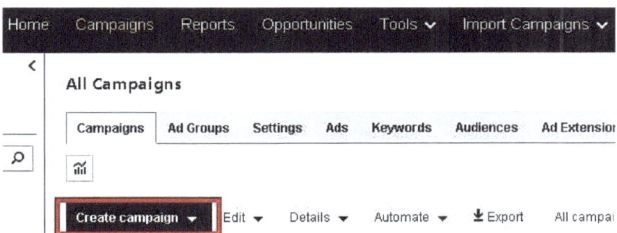

Next, we want to fill out our campaign as follows:

Next, you will see the ad copy being requested:

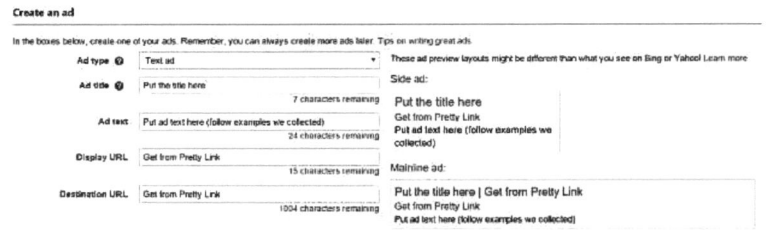

One thing to note is that for the two URL's, the display URL and destination URL, the links must be the same base domain.

For example, the following is acceptable:

Display URL: www.example.com

Destination URL: www.example.com/page1

Once this campaign is accepted, you will want to pause the campaign immediately so we can change our keyword bids.

Follow these images to change the keyword bids and set your bids to .05-.10:

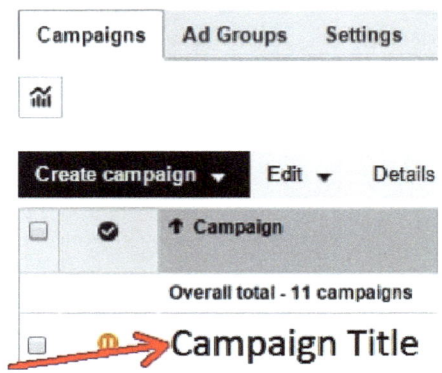

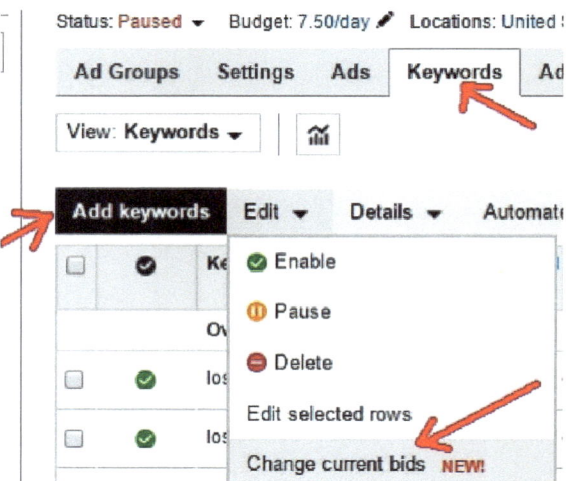

There are two more things we need to do.

The first is insert more ads. Head here:

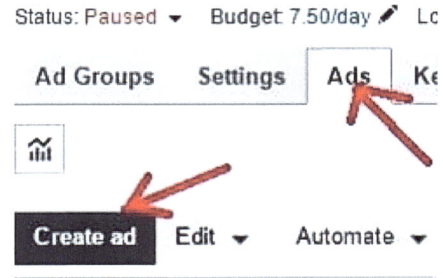

Now, once you have a minimum of 4 and a maximum of 7 ads, we are ready for the last step, which is tweaking gender information/ age information.

If you want to target just women or people of a certain age, do it here:

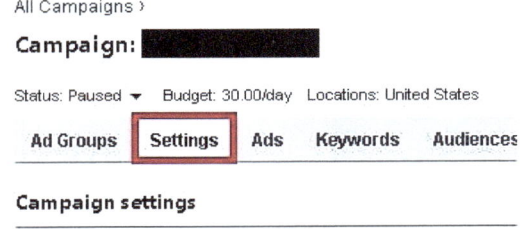

Tweak the bids for men or women or people of certain ages by decreasing them.

If you want no men, decrease the male bid by 90%, you get the picture.
Here's an example:

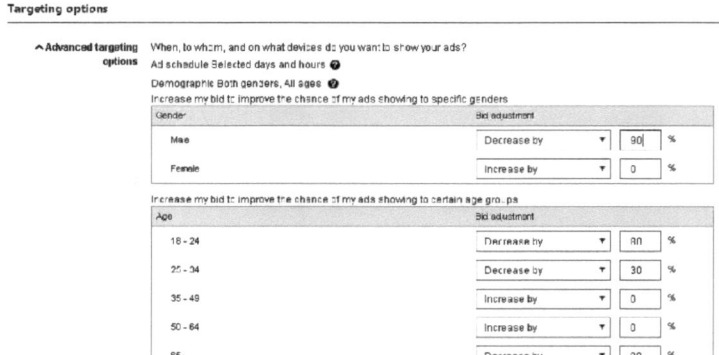

Now, double check that all your keyword bids are .05-.10, double check all your ads are in and all your links work, and then let your commission machine go!

Campaign Monitoring and Optimization

So now your first ad has been running for around 24-48 hours.

If for some reason you're not seeing any stats on your ads after this amount of time, you will need to contact chat support, something is wrong with the ad.

Otherwise, we should now have a good amount of impressions, and hopefully a good amount of clicks!

This is how we will measure it. The first number to look at is impressions. These are how many times your ads were displayed. The next number to look at is your total clicks, followed by your CTR (click through rate).

The click through rate is what percent of people clicked divided by the total number of times the ad was displayed.

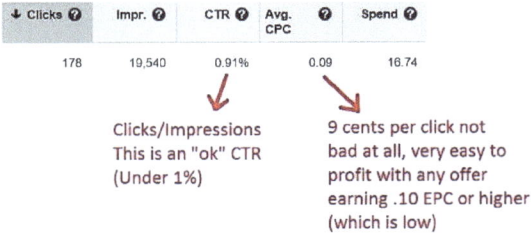

We can monitor our campaigns to see how they are performing.

If you have spent as much as a commission payout, for example an offer you're promoting in one of your machines pays out $35 and you've spent $30-$35 with no sale, it's time to pause the campaign.
You can either try again with new keywords, or work on new offers. If you've tried an offer with over 3 different

keyword sets and it isn't converting, it's probably time to move on to another offer.

If you have very low clicks, it means you need to check that your ads are highly relevant to your keywords. Change up ads before pausing a campaign to see if you can improve the click through rate.

Other than that, if you're tracking, you can see which keywords are bringing you the sale in funnel flux.

From the main page, go to Statistics → Drill Down Reports

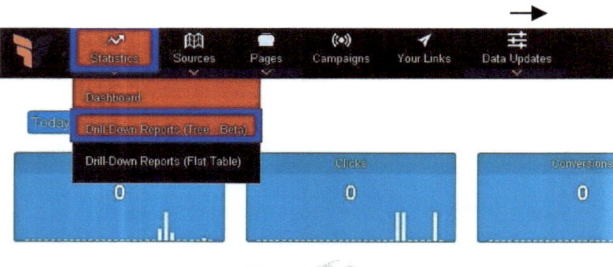

Next, select the following fields, in this order:

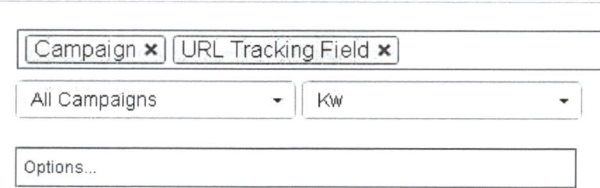

Choose the campaign that you want to check and select "Kw" for the URL tracking field.

A list of keywords will popup. Green is for positive ROI keywords and red is for 40 negative.

You can also check out other results like these.

So you can modify your campaigns based on these variables.

How to succeed with this method.

We have done everything in our power to ensure the highest chance of profitability with our campaigns.

One thing to remember is that unfortunately, it's impossible to be profitable with every single campaign.

So, there is a certain way you need to approach this.

Aim to put up a certain amount of commission machines at a time.

For example, if you want to be aggressive, aim for 20 commission machines per week. A certain percentage of these will be profitable. It can be 2 of them , or it can be 15 of them.

Over time, you will be able to accumulate many that are profitable.

This is where strength in numbers come in.

Know that the power of this method is the ability to get super cheap clicks that won't break your budget, and help you achieve massive ROI.

Since you can do this with any campaign in any niche, you have the ability to 41 have potentially 100 or more profitable campaigns going in just a few weeks from now.

Even if each one is only making you $20-$30 per day in profit, that's another $2000-$3000

The more you stay diligent, the more super profitable campaigns you will finding some cases 10,000% ROI.

Long story short, keep going. Eventually you can have 500 machines running then you're a five figure per month affiliate marketer.

All you need is a plan and diligence.

This is what you'll get with this method. Just remember to test, test, and test.

Kill the losers and scale the winners.

Some variables work against you, but remember, this is a hell of a lot easier and quicker than 10 years in the corporate world to work up to 6 figures a year.

Stay diligent and you will crush it.

Outsourcing

Eventually, you may want to outsource your keyword research, ad copy research, offer research, or campaign setup.

This would let you really scale things up down the road. A great place to hire people cheap is www.upwork.com where you can hire someone for as low as $3-$5 per hour to do certain tasks for you.

It's important to remember to be diligent.

You're not necessarily going to find a superstar employee on the first try.

However, once you find an awesome employee, you'll be able to scale up big time.

Once you create an Upwork account, simply post up a new job. You can use titles like
"New Bing ads employee needed"

There will be many people applying that want to work for $5-$10 per hour.

Make sure you see that they have good reviews, and say you are happy to hire them if they are willing to work on a trial period for $2 or $3 per hour (unless you feel like paying more)

I have found that doing this increases their will to work, and lets you test them out without breaking the bank.

Conclusion

So now you know how to set up your commission machines.

Remember, this is a number's game. Set a goal and keep going.

Don't get discouraged if many campaigns fail- keep going.

You can see results with this as soon as you set up your first machine.

You can try with or without tracking, and switch off as you please.

For now, enjoy your Funnel Affiliates!

Resources

www.funnelflux.com

www.bingads.com

www.upwork.com

www.follow.net

www.ispionage.com

www.neilpatel.com/ubersuggest

www.ingramcontent.com/pod-product-compliance
Lightning Source LLC
Chambersburg PA
CBHW040336220526
45473CB00009B/2703